Curious George®

Farm to Table

Adaptation by Julie M. Fenner
Based on the TV series teleplay written by Ken Scarborough

Houghton Mifflin Harcourt
Boston   New York

ISBN: 978-0-544-65220-0 paper over board
ISBN: 978-0-544-65222-4 paperback
Design by Afsoon Razavi
Illustrations adapted by Rudy and Kaci Obrero
www.hmhco.com
Printed in China
SCP 10 9 8 7 6 5 4 3 2 1
4500585812

George was helping his friend Marco make his famous tortillas for his abuela's birthday dinner.

George reached for a bag on the windowsill, but it accidentally fell to the ground! "Don't worry, George," said Marco, "that's the masa, or cornmeal. We use it to make tortillas. I'm sure we have more."

Marco looked in the cupboard.

"Uh, oh. I *thought* we had more," he said.

George had an idea. He knew exactly where they could find the masa Marco needed.

They walked to the local grocery store and asked the store clerk.
"Masa? Oh, I'm sorry. I just sold the last bag."
"But I promised my grandmother I would make tortillas for her birthday," said Marco.

Beep! Beep!
"You're in luck! The delivery man is here," said the store clerk.
"My Uncle Enrique!" Marco exclaimed. "Let's ask him for more masa."

"Uncle Enrique! Today is Abuela's birthday. I want to make her tortillas, but I don't have any masa," said Marco.
"No masa! I don't have any on my truck, but I know where we can get some," said Uncle Enrique.

"My job is to deliver food from the warehouse to the grocery store," Uncle Enrique explained. "Let's drive to the warehouse to get more masa."

Unfortunately, the warehouse manager said they did not have any masa. "I'm waiting for a shipment. But hold on . . ."

She took them to a different part of the warehouse.
"You might find one bag up there," she said, pointing to the top shelf.

Luckily, George was an expert climber.
When he reached the top, he saw the masa.
George had saved the day!

With the bag tucked under his arm, George started to climb down the shelf.
"Wait, George. Toss the masa to me," shouted Uncle Enrique. "I'll catch it!"
George tossed the bag.

Just then the warehouse manager yelled, "Watch out!" to another employee.
Distracted, Uncle Enrique looked away and the bag fell to the ground and burst open.

As they left the warehouse, Uncle Enrique said, "I'm sorry, Marco. Abuela won't have tortillas for her birthday. It's all my fault." They climbed back into the delivery truck.

George looked at the back of the empty bag. He pointed to the picture.
"George, you're right! That's the mill where they make the masa. There's
even an address, and it's not too far away," said Uncle Enrique.
They decided to drive to the mill.

Inside the mill, a worker showed them how masa is made.
"Grains like corn and wheat come into the mill and are cleaned and inspected. Then the grains are put into a grinder and come out as cornmeal or flour. Next it is sifted to remove the parts we don't need. Finally, the cornmeal or flour is bagged and shipped to the warehouse."

"Could we have one bag of masa?" asked Uncle Enrique.
"I'm sorry. Our corn comes from local farmers, but there wasn't enough rain
this year and the drought delayed the corn harvest. No corn, no masa."

George knew a local farmer who grew corn. He even stored rainwater for his crops!
George pointed the way to the Renkinses' farm.

"Thanks to my water tank, we stored enough
water to get through the season. I harvested
corn all day today," said Farmer Renkins. Farmer Renkins was happy to help.
He gave them fresh and dried corn.

They took the dried corn to the mill, where it was ground into masa and put into bags. While Uncle Enrique took the bags to the warehouse to be packaged for the grocery stores, George and Marco took one bag home to make tortillas.

George now understood that the food in the stores came from farmers like his friend Mr. Renkins!

At last, Marco was able to make his famous tortillas for his abuela's birthday dinner. The whole family loved them. George did too!

Green Thumb

George and Marco learned that the masa in the grocery store comes from corn grown by farmers like Mr. Renkins. Test your green thumb by creating your own mini greenhouse.

You will need . . .
egg carton (only the bottom), soil, vegetable seeds, water, plastic wrap, or a clear plastic bag

What to do:

1. Fill each egg slot with soil.

2. Place one seed into each slot. Make sure the seed is covered with soil.

3. Water each seed so that the soil is damp but not watery.

4. Cover with plastic wrap or a clear plastic bag and set on a sunny windowsill. If the soil starts to look dry, uncover the carton and add water.

5. Wait and check for little green sprouts!

6. Once the plants are big enough, transfer them to a larger container or a garden.

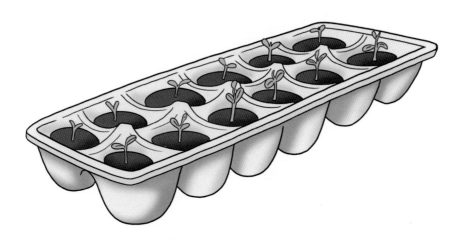

Foods from Nature

Marco created his famous tortillas using cornmeal made from ground corn. Many fruits and vegetables are used to create other foods. For example, apples are cooked and mashed for applesauce and grapes are dried to make raisins. Can you think of other fruits and vegetables that can be used to create different foods? Ask a family member or friend for more suggestions.

Five Food Groups

Did you know there are five food groups? They are . . .

grains and starches   **vegetables**   **fruits**   **dairy**   **protein (meat and fish)**

Corn is part of the grain and starch food group. Grains and starches include pastas, breads, rice, cereals, and beans. Starchy vegetables, such as corn and potatoes, are also considered grains and starches. Can you guess which food groups the items pictured below belong to?

Answers:
grains: bread
vegetables: broccoli, carrot
fruits: apple, banana
dairy: milk, cheese
protein: chicken